Fruit & Vegetables
IN CROSS STITCH

Angela Beazley

MEREHURST

For my mother, who first kindled my enthusiasm

THE CHARTS

Some of the designs in this book are very detailed and, due to inevitable space limitations, the charts may be shown on a comparatively small scale; in such cases, readers may find it helpful to have the particular chart with which they are currently working enlarged.

THREADS

The projects in this book were all stitched with DMC stranded cotton embroidery threads. The keys given with each chart also list thread combinations for those who wish to use Anchor or Madeira threads. It should be pointed out that the shades produced by different companies vary slightly, and it is not always possible to find identical colours in a different range.

Published in 1995 by Merehurst Limited
Ferry House, 51-57 Lacy Road, Putney, London SW15 1PR
Copyright © 1995 Merehurst Limited
ISBN 1 85391 446 0

A catalogue record for this book is available from the British Library.

Commissioning Editor Cheryl Brown
Edited by Heather Dewhurst
Designed by Maggie Aldred
Photography by Marie-Louise Avery
Illustrations by John Hutchinson
Typesetting by Dacorum Type & Print, Hemel Hempstead
Colour separation by Fotographics Limited, UK – Hong Kong
Printed in Hong Kong by Wing King Tong

Merehurst is the leading publisher of craft books and has an excellent range of titles to suit all levels. Please send to the address above for our free catalogue, stating the title of this book.

CONTENTS

Introduction   4

Basic Skills   4

Recipe Book Cover and Bookmark   8

Strawberry Garland Table Set   12

Cafetière Cover and Pot Stand   16

Cornucopia Picture   20

Apple Trellis Bag   24

Vegetable Garden Sampler   28

Fruit Garden Sampler   32

Fruity Cushion   36

Citrus Kitchen Towel   40

Vegetable Tea Towel   44

Acknowledgements and Suppliers   48

INTRODUCTION

Cross stitch is a form of embroidery that has become more and more popular in recent times for the decoration of household linen and furnishings. It is very easy to learn and, once you have mastered the few basic skills, you can attempt any design. Fruit and vegetables in all their varied colours and shapes are the themes of this book. So whether you like apples and strawberries or sweetcorn and peppers, there is a design to appeal to everyone's taste. The projects offered include tea towels, samplers, a table set and cushion, in addition to a bookmark and pot stand.

Each cross stitch design is carefully charted and has an accompanying colour key and full instructions for making up the project. Also included is a Basic Skills section, which covers everything from how to prepare your fabric and stretch it in an embroidery hoop or frame, to mounting your cross stitch embroidery over cardboard, ready for display.

Some of the designs in this book are very simple and are aimed at beginners, such as the Citrus Kitchen Towel. Others are more challenging and are suitable for the more experienced stitcher or for those eager to expand their skills, such as the Fruit and Vegetable Garden Samplers.

Whatever your level of skill or interest in cross stitch, I hope you will enjoy being able to create items from the wide range of projects offered in this book.

BASIC SKILLS

BEFORE YOU BEGIN

PREPARING THE FABRIC
Even with an average amount of handling, many evenweave fabrics tend to fray at the edges, so it is a good idea to overcast the raw edges, using ordinary sewing thread, before you begin.

THE INSTRUCTIONS
Each project begins with a full list of the materials that you will require; Aida and Linda are fabrics produced by Zweigart. Note that the measurements given for the embroidery fabric include a minimum of 3cm (1¹/₄in) all around to allow for stretching it in a frame and preparing the edges to prevent them from fraying.

Colour keys for stranded embroidery cottons – DMC, Anchor or Madeira – are given with each chart. It is assumed that you will need to buy one skein of each colour mentioned in a particular key, even though you may use less, but where two or more skeins are needed, this information is included in the main list of requirements.

To work from the charts, particularly those where several symbols are used in close proximity, some readers may find it helpful to have the chart enlarged so that the squares and symbols can be seen more easily. Many photocopying services will do this for a minimum charge.

Before you begin to embroider, always mark the centre of the design with two lines of basting stitches, one vertical and one horizontal, running from edge to edge of the fabric, as indicated by the arrows on the charts.

As you stitch, use the centre lines given on the chart and the basting threads on your fabric as reference points for counting the squares and threads to position your design accurately.

WORKING IN A HOOP
A hoop is the most popular frame for use with small areas of embroidery. It consists of two rings, one fitted inside the other; the outer ring usually has an adjustable screw attachment so that it can be tightened to hold the stretched fabric in place. Hoops are available in several sizes, ranging from

10cm (4in) in diameter to quilting hoops with a diameter of 38cm (15in). Hoops with table stands or floor stands attached are also available.

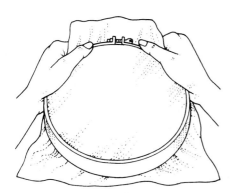

1 To stretch your fabric in a hoop, place the area to be embroidered over the inner ring and press the outer ring over it, with the tension screw released. Tissue paper can be placed between the outer ring and the embroidery, so that the hoop does not mark the fabric. Lay the tissue paper over the fabric when you set it in the hoop, then tear away the central embroidery area.

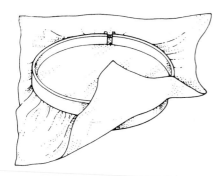

2 Smooth the fabric and, if necessary, straighten the grain before tightening the screw. The fabric should be evenly stretched.

EXTENDING EMBROIDERY FABRIC

It is easy to extend a piece of embroidery fabric, such as a bookmark, to stretch it in a hoop.

● Fabric oddments of a similar weight can be used. Simply cut four pieces to size (in other words, to the measurement that will fit both the embroidery fabric

and your hoop) and baste them to each side of the embroidery fabric before stretching it in the hoop in the usual way.

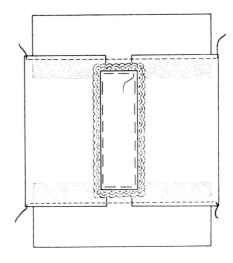

WORKING IN A RECTANGULAR FRAME

Rectangular frames are more suitable for larger pieces of embroidery. They consist of two rollers, with tapes attached, and two flat side pieces, which slot into the rollers and are held in place by pegs or screw attachments. Available in different sizes, either alone or with adjustable table or floor stands, frames are measured by the length of the roller tape, and range in size from 30cm (12in) to 68cm (27in).

As alternatives to a slate frame, canvas stretchers and the backs of old picture frames can be used. Provided there is sufficient extra fabric around the finished size of the embroidery, the edges can be turned under and simply attached with drawing pins (thumb tacks) or staples.

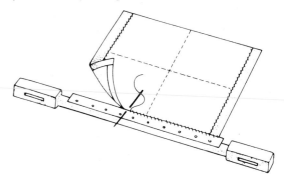

1 To stretch your fabric in a rectangular frame, cut out the fabric, allowing at least an extra 5cm (2in) all around the finished size of the embroidery. Baste a single 12mm (½in) turning on the top and bottom edges and oversew strong tape, 2.5cm (1in) wide, to the other two sides. Mark the centre line both ways with basting stitches. Working from the centre outwards and using strong thread, oversew the top and bottom edges to the roller tapes. Fit the side pieces into the slots, and roll any extra fabric on one roller until the fabric is taut.

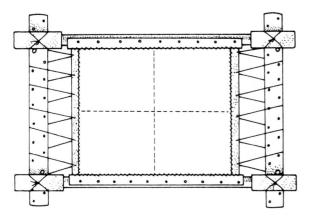

2 Insert the pegs or adjust the screw attachments to secure the frame. Thread a large-eyed needle (chenille needle) with strong thread or fine string and lace both edges, securing the ends around the intersections of the frame. Lace the webbing at 2.5cm (1in) intervals, stretching the fabric evenly.

MITRING A CORNER
Press a single hem to the wrong side, the same as the measurement given in the instructions. Open the hem out again and fold the corner of the fabric inwards as shown on the diagram. Refold the hem to the wrong side along the pressed line, and slip-stitch in place.

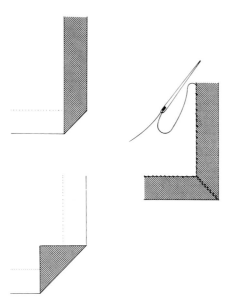

MOUNTING EMBROIDERY
The cardboard should be cut to the size of the finished embroidery, with an extra 6mm ('/₄in) added all round to allow for the recess in the frame.

LIGHTWEIGHT FABRICS

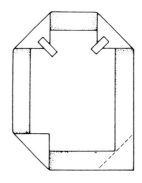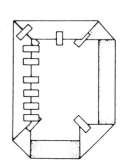

1 Place embroidery face down, with the cardboard centred on top, and basting and pencil lines matching. Begin by folding over the fabric at each corner and securing it with masking tape.

2 Working first on one side and then the other, fold over the fabric on all sides and secure it firmly with pieces of masking tape, placed about 2.5cm (1in) apart. Also neaten the mitred corners with masking tape, pulling the fabric tightly to give a firm, smooth finish.

HEAVIER FABRICS

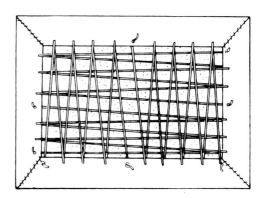

● Lay the embroidery face down, with the cardboard centred on top; fold over the edges of the fabric on opposite sides, making mitred folds at the corners, and lace across, using strong thread. Repeat on the other two sides. Finally, pull up the fabric firmly over the cardboard. Overstitch the mitred corners.

CROSS STITCH

For all cross stitch embroidery, the following two methods of working are used. In each case, neat rows of vertical stitches are produced on the back of the fabric.

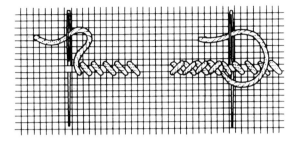

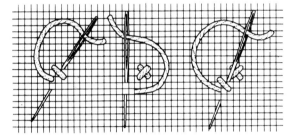

● When stitching large areas, work in horizontal rows. Working from right to left, complete the first row of evenly spaced diagonal stitches over the number of threads specified in the project instructions. Then, working from left to right, repeat the process. Continue in this way, making sure each stitch crosses in the same direction.

● When stitching diagonal lines, work downwards, completing each stitch before moving to the next.

BACKSTITCH

Backstitch is used in the projects to give emphasis to a particular foldline, an outline or a shadow. The stitches are worked over the same number of threads as the cross stitch, forming continuous straight or diagonal lines.

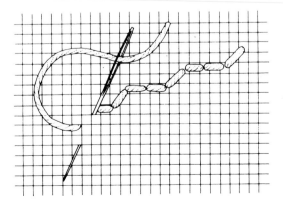

● Make the first stitch from left to right; pass the needle behind the fabric and bring it out one stitch length ahead to the left. Repeat and continue in this way along the line.

HALF CROSS STITCHES

Some fractional stitches are used on certain projects in this book; although they strike fear into the hearts of less experienced stitchers they are not difficult to master, and give a more natural line in certain instances. Should you find it difficult to pierce the centre of the Aida block, simply use a sharp needle to make a small hole in the centre first.

To work a half cross, bring the needle up at point A and down through the centre of the square at B. Later, the diagonal back stitch finishes the stitch. A chart square with two different symbols separated by a diagonal line requires two half stitches. Backstitch will later finish the square.

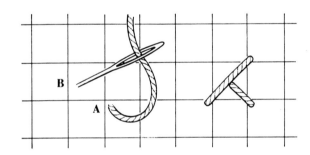

FRENCH KNOTS

To work a french knot, bring your needle and cotton out slightly to the right of where you want your knot to be. Wind the thread once around the needle and insert the needle to the left of the point where you brought it out.

Be careful not to pull too hard or the knot will disappear through the fabric.

Recipe Book Cover and Bookmark

What better way to decorate a treasured recipe book than with a design of vegetables? And to extend the theme, you can mark the page of a favourite recipe with a bookmark embroidered with mushrooms.

RECIPE BOOK COVER
AND BOOKMARK

YOU WILL NEED

For the Recipe Book, measuring
19cm × 27cm (7½in × 10¾in):

54cm × 41.5cm (21½in × 16½in) sand-coloured
14-count Aida fabric
Stranded embroidery cotton in the colours given in
the panel
No24 tapestry needle
Sticky tape
Fabric glue
26.5cm × 19cm (10½in × 7½in) fabric for
inner cover
Matching sewing thread

For the Bookmark, measuring 22.5cm × 6.5cm
(9in × 2½in):

30cm (12in) length of Aida band, 28 blocks wide,
with red scalloped edge
Stranded embroidery cotton in the colours given in
the panel
No24 tapestry needle
Matching sewing thread

•

THE EMBROIDERY

To alter the size of the book cover to fit a book of your choice, simply calculate the amount of fabric required as follows: first measure the width and height of the book. Then add together the width of the book twice, plus the width of the spine, plus 15cm (6in) for turnings – this figure is the width of fabric required. To calculate the length, simply add 15cm (6in) to the height of the book.

Prepare the fabric for the recipe book cover by marking the lines of the design area with basting stitches (see the diagram) and mounting the fabric in a hoop or frame as shown on pages 4-5. Following the chart, start to embroider from the centre of the design panel, using two strands of cotton in the needle for cross stitch and french knots, and one strand for backstitch.

For the bookmark, begin the embroidery 7.5cm (3in) from the top of the fabric. Gently steam press the finished embroideries on the wrong side.

RECIPE BOOK COVER ▶		DMC	ANCHOR	MADEIRA
•	White	White	White	White
V	Ecru	Ecru	387	Ecru
⟍	Brown	840	379	1912
=	Purple	3740	872	806
L	Green	937	268	1504
T	Light green	3348	264	1409
R	Red	349	13	0212
C	Light orange	922	337	0310
X	Dark orange	921	338	0311
A	Blue green	501	878	1704
⋀	Dark blue green	500	879	1705
S	Golden brown	435	901	2010
■	Dark golden brown	436	363	2011
N	Mushroom	842	376	1910
B	Dark brown	433	371	2008
O	Blue	931	921	1711

Note: backstitch around mushrooms in brown, the onions in dark golden brown and the leaves in light green. Work the french knots (shown on chart by black circle) in purple.

MAKING UP THE BOOK COVER

Place the fabric embroidered-side down and lay the open book centrally on the top. Trim the fabric edges so that they extend 3.5cm (1⅜in) all around the book edges. Beginning with the inside front cover, fold the fabric onto the book and secure in place with strips of sticky tape, mitring the corners as shown on page 6. Slit the excess fabric at the spine edge and fold the resulting thin piece of fabric down inside the spine. Dab a small amount of glue on the raw edge of this piece of fabric to prevent it fraying. Secure the fabric on the back cover as for the front. Slip stitch all corners to keep the fabric firmly in place.

Cut two pieces of fabric the size of the book front and machine stitch a 12mm (½in) hem around all edges. Place one of the pieces of fabric wrong side down over the inside cover to conceal the sticky tape and the raw edge at the spine. Slip stitch in place. Repeat for the inside back cover.

COMPLETING THE BOOKMARK

Turn under a 12mm (½in) hem at the top of the bookmark, then turn the fabric again to hide the raw edge. Slip stitch in place with matching thread.

Trim the lower edge of the bookmark to form a 'V'-shape, and make a 12mm (½in) slit up the centre. Turn the raw edges up by 12mm (½in) on the wrong side, and trim away the excess fabric at the centre. Turn up the fabric again to hide the raw edges and slip stitch in place with matching thread.

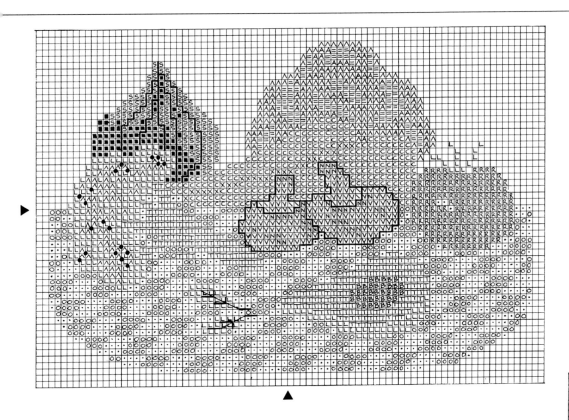

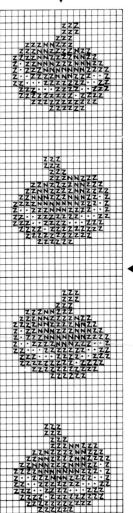

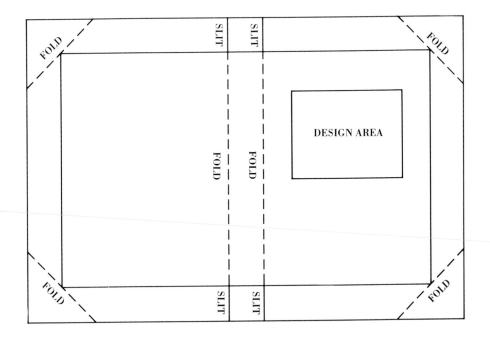

SLIT SLIT

FOLD FOLD

FOLD FOLD

FOLD

DESIGN AREA

FOLD FOLD

SLIT SLIT

BOOKMARK ▶		DMC	ANCHOR	MADEIRA
Z	Mushroom	613	853	2109
•	Ecru	Ecru	387	Ecru
N	Brown	611	898	2107

Strawberry Garland Table Set

Perfect for a summer lunch party, the twining strawberry design of this table set adds a touch of distinction to a plain tablecloth, while the matching serviette holders complete the fruity look.

STRAWBERRY GARLAND TABLE SET

YOU WILL NEED

For the Tablecloth, measuring 103cm (41¼in) square:

1m (40in) square pink 25-count evenweave fabric
Matching sewing thread
Stranded embroidery cotton in the colours given in the panel
No24 tapestry needle
425cm (170in) white lace, 2cm (¾in) wide, for edging

For the Serviette Holders, each measuring 4.5cm × 4.5cm (1¾in × 1¾in):

Oddments of white 18-count Aida fabric
Stranded embroidery cotton in the colours given in the panel
No24 tapestry needle
Serviette holders (for suppliers, see page 48)

•

THE TABLECLOTH

Prepare the fabric by machine zigzag stitching around the edges to prevent it fraying. Mark the centre of the fabric with lines of horizontal and vertical basting stitches and mount the fabric in a hoop or frame as shown on pages 4-5. Following the chart, start to embroider from the centre of the design, marked M on the garland chart, using two strands of cotton in the needle and working over two threads of the fabric. Work the lower half of the garland first, then turn the fabric around through 180 degrees and complete the central design.

To position the corner motifs, baste diagonal lines outwards from the centre of the fabric. Count 100 stitches (200 threads of the fabric) from the outer edge of the garland to the letter C on the corner motif chart. Work the right hand motif first, then turn the chart 90 degrees clockwise, and position for the left hand corner in the same way. To embroider the remaining two corners, turn the fabric around through 180 degrees and repeat. Gently steam press the finished embroidery on the wrong side.

To finish the tablecloth, machine stitch white lace around the edges, making pleats at each corner.

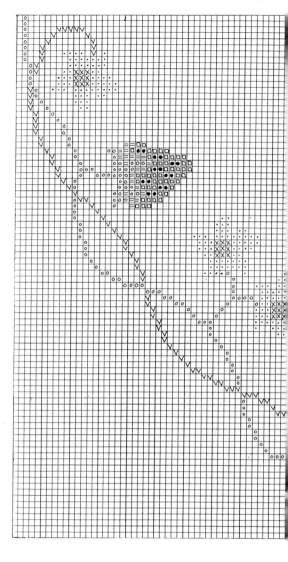

THE SERVIETTE HOLDERS

Mark the centre of each oddment of fabric with basting stitches and mount the fabric in a hoop or frame (see pages 4-5). Following the chart, embroider the motif, starting from the centre of the design and using one strand of cotton in the needle. Steam press the finished embroidery on the wrong side.

Trim the fabric to fit the serviette holder and slide it gently in position in the holder. Repeat to make the required number of serviette holders.

STRAWBERRY GARLAND TABLE SET ▲		DMC	ANCHOR	MADEIRA
·	White	White	White	White
V	Pale green	417	0265	1501
O	Dark green	3346	0267	1407
●	Pale yellow	744	0301	0112
X	Deep yellow	744	0305	0113
□	Red	321	013	0510
=	Deep red	498	047	0510

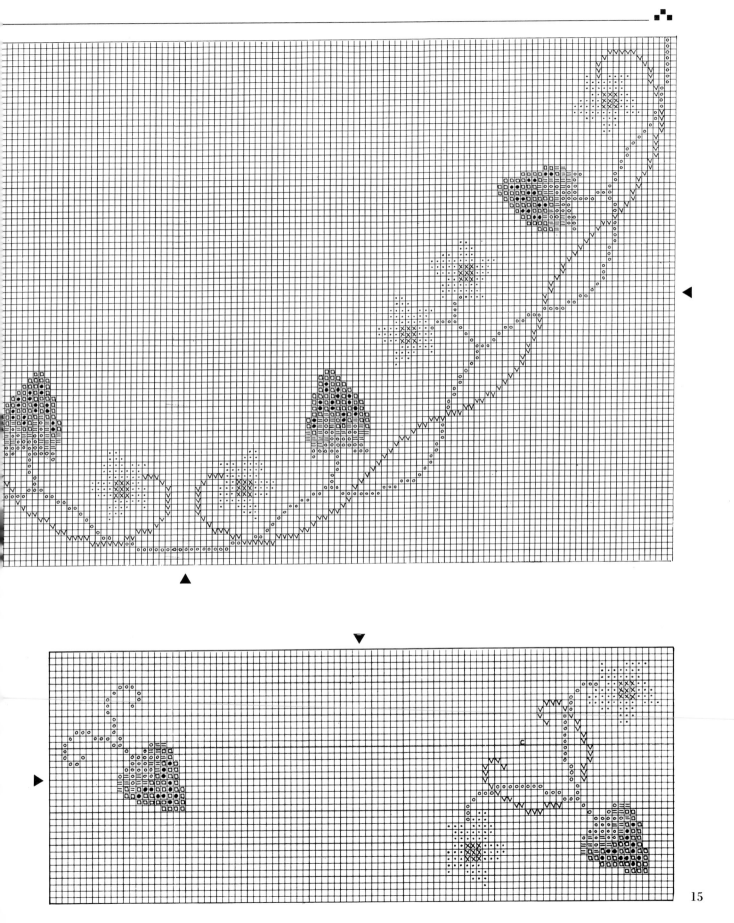

Cafetière Cover and Pot Stand

Give your kitchen a coordinated look with this pretty cafetière cover and matching pot stand. If desired, you could even use the design to stitch a picture for your wall.

CAFETIÈRE COVER AND POT STAND

CAFETIÈRE COVER ▶		DMC	ANCHOR	MADEIRA
P	Pink	776	24	0503
C	Pale yellow	744	301	0112
B	Purple	327	100	0805
O	Brownish red	315	896	0810
+	Dark green	987	244	1403
V	Pale green	471	265	1501
L	Olive green	3011	845	1607
•	Brown	610	889	2106
Y	Yellow	726	295	0100

Note: backstitch butterflies' antennae in brown. Attach beads using one strand of purple in the beading needle where the chart shows B.

YOU WILL NEED

For the Cafetière Cover, measuring 14.5cm × 40cm (5³⁄₄in × 16in):

29cm × 50cm (11¹⁄₂in × 20in) ivory 27-count evenweave fabric
Stranded embroidery cotton in the colours given in the panel
No24 tapestry needle
Beading needle
Metallic purple seed beads
13cm × 35.5cm (5¹⁄₄in × 14¹⁄₄in) white 60g (2oz) wadding (batting)
Touch-and-close fastener

For the Pot Stand, measuring 7.5cm (3in) in diameter:

12.5cm × 12.5cm (5in × 5in) ivory 27-count evenweave fabric
Stranded embroidery cotton in the colours given in the panel
No24 tapestry needle
Pot stand (for suppliers, see page 48)

•

THE EMBROIDERY

Machine zigzag stitch around the edges of the fabric to prevent fraying. Mark the centre of the fabric with horizontal and vertical lines of basting stitches (for the cafetière cover, the shorter sides of the fabric are the sides) and mount it in a hoop or frame as shown on pages 4-5. Following the chart, start to embroider from the centre of the design, using two strands of cotton in the needle for the cross stitches and working over two strands of fabric in each direction.

Work the backstitch details using one strand of cotton in the needle. To attach the beads on the cafetière cover, use one strand of purple in the beading needle and stitch the second step of a cross stitch, catching a bead with each stitch.

Gently steam press the finished embroideries on the wrong side.

MAKING THE CAFETIÈRE COVER

Trim the embroidered fabric so that it measures 49cm (19¹⁄₂in) wide. Lay the fabric embroidered-side down and place the wadding (batting) centrally on the top. Pin and baste it in place. Turn the short sides of the fabric over the wadding (batting), giving a finished width of 40cm (16in). Machine stitch along the sides, 12mm (¹⁄₂in) from the edge.

Turn the long edges of the fabric over the wadding (batting), giving a finished height of 14.5cm (5³⁄₄in). Where the fabric meets over the wadding (batting), make a 12mm (¹⁄₂in) turning to overlap the raw edges.

Machine straight stitch around all the sides of the cover, 6mm (¹⁄₄in) from the edge. Slip stitch the overlap at the back of the cover and press. Remove the basting stitches. Stick the touch-and-close fastener on the overlap at the back of the cover so that the cover fits the cafetière snugly.

COMPLETING THE POT STAND

Place the paper circle provided with the pot stand behind the embroidery and run a gathering thread around the fabric 6mm (¹⁄₄in) beyond the paper circle. Cut away the excess fabric 12mm (¹⁄₂in) beyond this line. Pull up the gathering thread gently until the paper is encased by the embroidery and place it in a glass stand so that the embroidery is adjacent to the glass in the dish shape. Peel off the sticky paper behind the green felt circle and place the felt over the flat edge of the pot stand. This will form the underside of the pot stand.

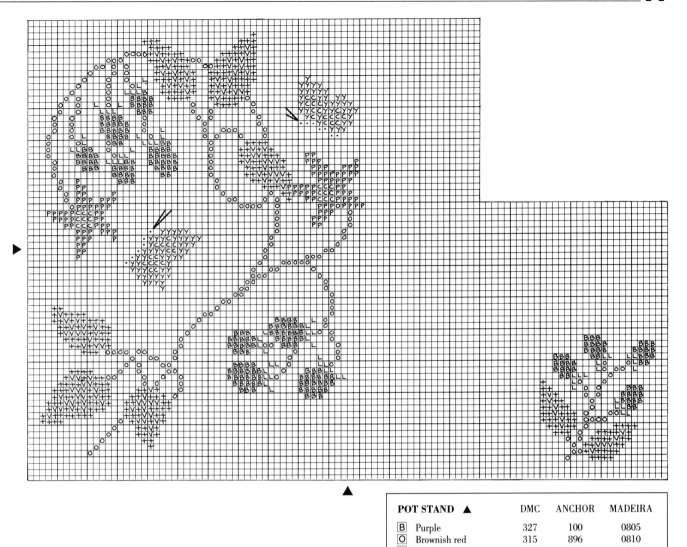

POT STAND ▲		DMC	ANCHOR	MADEIRA
B	Purple	327	100	0805
O	Brownish red	315	896	0810
+	Dark green	987	244	1403
V	Pale green	471	265	1501
L	Olive green	3C11	845	1607

DESIGN AREA

NB: **X** shows position of touch-and-close fastener

Cornucopia Picture

This design of the horn of plenty, overflowing with an abundance of fruit and vegetables, would make an ideal picture to hang in the kitchen.

CORNUCOPIA PICTURE

YOU WILL NEED

For the Cornucopia Picture, mounted in a rectangular landscape frame, with an aperture measuring 16.5cm × 12.5cm (6½in × 5in):

30cm × 25cm (12in × 10in) white
16-count Aida fabric
Stranded embroidery cotton in the colours given in the panel
No24 tapestry needle
Strong thread for lacing across the back
Stiff cardboard for mounting
Frame of your choice

●

THE EMBROIDERY

Prepare the fabric by marking the centre with lines of vertical and horizontal basting stitches and mounting in a hoop or frame as shown on pages 4-5. Following the chart, start to embroider from the centre of the design, using two strands of cotton in the needle. Gently steam press the finished embroidery on the wrong side.

ASSEMBLING THE PICTURE

Trim the edges of the embroidery and centre the picture over the cardboard mount. Lace the embroidery over the mount, following the instructions on page 6. Complete the assembly of the frame according to the manufacturer's instructions.

CORNUCOPIA PICTURE ▶		DMC	ANCHOR	MADEIRA
V	Gold	729	890	2209
A	Dark gold	781	309	2213
S	Dark blue	930	922	1712
+	Purple	3740	872	3041
R	Red	304	47	0509
X	Green	3347	266	1408
O	Dark blue green	500	879	1705
C	Blue green	501	878	1704
•	White	White	White	White
＼	Pale yellow green	734	279	1610
Y	Yellow	726	295	0100
P	Dark yellow green	733	280	1611
B	Brown	3790	903	2106
⊥	Bright green	3346	267	1407
=	Orange	721	324	0308
‖	Dark orange	720	326	0309

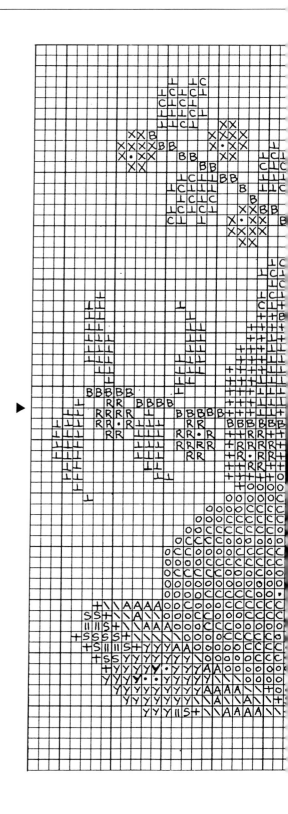

Apple Trellis Bag

This stylish cross stitch design
features a pattern of apples
surrounded by a trellis latticework.
The bag can be used as a clutch bag
or purse, or even a make-up bag.

VEGETABLE GARDEN SAMPLER

YOU WILL NEED

For the Vegetable Garden Sampler, mounted in a rectangular portrait frame with an aperture measuring 35cm × 31.5cm (14in × 12½in):

50cm × 50cm (20in × 20in) antique white 28-count evenweave fabric
Stranded embroidery cotton in the colours given in the panel
No24 tapestry needle
Strong thread for lacing across the back
Stiff cardboard for mounting
Frame of your choice

●

THE EMBROIDERY

Prepare the fabric by marking the centre with lines of vertical and horizontal basting stitches and then mounting it in a hoop or frame as shown on pages 4-5. Following the chart, start to embroider from the centre of the design, using two strands of cotton in the needle for cross stitches and french knots unless otherwise specified. Work the backstitch details using only one strand of cotton in the needle, unless otherwise specified. Refer to the diagram for how to work the half cross stitches. Gently steam press the finished embroidery on the wrong side.

ASSEMBLING THE PICTURE

Trim the edges of the embroidery and centre the picture over the cardboard mount. Lace the embroidery over the mount, following the instructions on page 6. Complete the assembly of the frame according to the manufacturer's instructions.

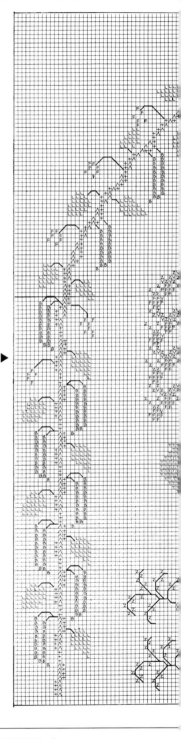

Where you see this

Stitch like this

● Yellow 726
◯ Terracotta 921
◌ Pale green 471

VEGETABLE GARDEN SAMPLER ▲				
		DMC	ANCHOR	MADEIRA
Λ	Brown	610	889	2106
+	Vine green	704	238	1308
B	Bean green	703	239	1307
L	Leaf green	702	226	1306
F	Red	349	13	0212
T	Orange	922	337	0310
Z	Deep green	3346	267	1407
R	Dark brown	840	379	1912

		DMC	ANCHOR	MADEIRA
V	Pale green	471	265	1501
N	Pale grey	415	398	1803
C	Terracotta	921	338	0311
	Yellow	726	295	0100
O	Blue	828	158	1101
•	White	White	White	White
	Dark grey	535	273	1809

Note: backstitch stems on bean arch in leaf green; the bunny tails in dark brown; the cauliflower in pale green (using two strands of cotton); the greenhouse (building) in dark grey; and the lettuce and stems on all greenhouse plants in deep green. Work french knots on yellow flowers in yellow, and bunny eyes in dark grey (using one strand of cotton).

Fruit Garden Sampler

This delightful sampler celebrating the glory of the fruit garden, can be made either on its own or as a pair with the Vegetable Garden Sampler, and used to decorate your kitchen.

FRUIT GARDEN SAMPLER

YOU WILL NEED

For the Fruit Garden Sampler, mounted in a rectangular portrait frame with an aperture measuring 35cm × 31.5cm (14in × 12½in):

50cm × 50cm (20in × 20in) antique white 28-count evenweave fabric
Stranded embroidery cotton in the colours given in the panel
No24 tapestry needle
Strong thread for lacing across the back
Stiff cardboard for mounting
Frame of your choice

•

THE EMBROIDERY

Prepare the fabric by marking the centre with lines of vertical and horizontal basting stitches and then mounting it in a hoop or frame as shown on pages 4-5. Following the chart, start to embroider from the centre of the design, using two strands of cotton in the needle for cross stitches. Work the backstitch details using only one strand of cotton in the needle. Refer to the diagram for how to work the half cross stitches. Gently steam press the finished embroidery on the wrong side.

ASSEMBLING THE PICTURE

Trim the edges of the embroidery and centre the picture over the cardboard mount. Lace the embroidery over the mount, following the instructions on page 6. Complete the assembly of the frame according to the manufacturer's instructions.

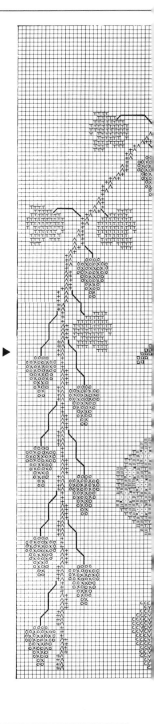

FRUIT GARDEN SAMPLER ▶		DMC	ANCHOR	MADEIRA				DMC	ANCHOR	MADEIRA
O	White	White	White	White		X	Light purple	554	97	0711
P	Pale blue	828	158	1101		+	Bright green	704	238	1308
B	Stone	422	943	2102		=	Light green	3347	266	1408
F	Dark stone	435	901	2010		T	Dark green	3346	267	1407
C	Terracotta	921	338	0311		•	Red	304	47	0509
E	Light terracotta	3776	349	2306		●	Pear	832	907	2202
V	Coffee	436	363	2011		▽	Black	310	403	Black
∧	Brown	840	379	1912						
□	Grey	3799	236	1713			*Note: backstitch stems in dark green, and the bird in grey.*				
O	Purple	552	99	0713						

Where you see this   Stitch like this   Where you see this   Stitch like this

◀ BIRD'S BEAK   ⋀ Brown 840

◀ PEAR TREES   ● Pear 832
                = Light green 3347

◀ APPLE TREES   · Red 304
                 = Light green 3347

Fruity Cushion

This brightly coloured cushion is simple to make and will add a pretty touch to any living room. If you prefer, you could stitch the design as a picture to hang on the wall of your dining room or kitchen.

FRUITY CUSHION

YOU WILL NEED

For the Fruity Cushion, measuring
35cm (14in) square:

*45cm (18in) square grey-blue 28-count
evenweave fabric
Stranded embroidery cotton in the colours
given in the panel
No24 tapestry needle
Matching sewing thread
45cm (18in) square plain or patterned fabric, for
cushion back
35cm (14in) square cushion pad
2m (2¹/₄yd) pearl grey silk cushion cord, 6mm (¹/₄in)
in diameter*

•

THE EMBROIDERY

Prepare the fabric, marking the centre with horizontal and vertical lines of basting stitches, and mount it in a hoop as shown on pages 4-5. Following the chart, start to embroider from the centre of the design, using two strands of cotton in the needle for cross stitches (except for the gold thread where you need only one strand), and working over two threads of fabric in each direction. Work the backstitch details using one strand of cotton in the needle. Gently steam press the finished embroidery on the wrong side.

MAKING UP THE COVER

Keeping the design centred, trim the fabric to measure 37cm (14³/₄in). Machine zigzag stitch the raw edges to prevent fraying. With right sides together, stitch the front and back pieces of the cushion cover together, taking a 1.5cm (⁵/₈in) seam allowance, and leaving an opening of 23cm (9¹/₄in) on one side. Turn the cover right side out and press. Insert the cushion pad and slip stitch the opening closed. Trim the edge of the cushion with the cushion cord, making a 13cm (5¹/₂in) loop at each corner, and slip stitch it in place.

For a fuller cushion, reduce the size of the cover by 1.5cm (⁵/₈in) all around.

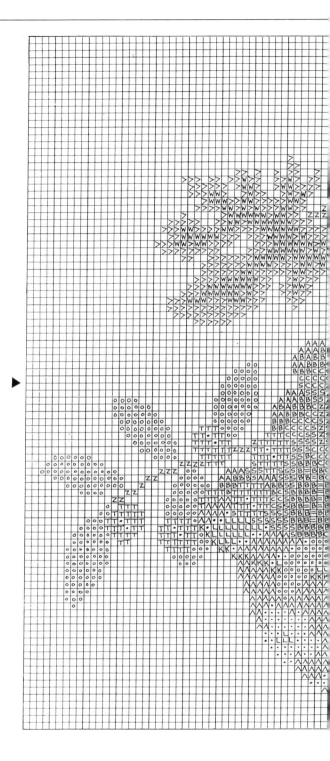

FRUITY CUSHION ▲		DMC	ANCHOR	MADEIRA				DMC	ANCHOR	MADEIRA
•	White	White	White	White		V	Old gold	734	279	1610
Λ	Pale blue	813	0160	1019		■	Dark old gold	832	0907	2202
L	Deep blue	312	0979	1005		>	Avocado green	470	0266	1502
C	Dark purple	552	0100	0713		W	Dark avocado green	469	0267	1503
B	Medium purple	553	098	0712		D	Pale green	989	0256	1401
A	Light purple	554	096	0711		P	Mid green	988	0257	1402
T	Red	321	013	0510		O	Dark green	987	0258	1403
S	Very dark purple	550	0101	0714		K	Light gold (metallic)		ART.282	
▢	Deep grey	3799	236	1713						
Z	Brown	869	0944	2105			*Note: backstitch the stems in dark green.*			

Citrus Kitchen Towel

Add a touch of zest to your washing
up with this kitchen towel decorated
with lemons and limes. This project
is quick and easy to stitch and would
be ideal for beginners.

CITRUS KITCHEN TOWEL

YOU WILL NEED

For the Citrus Kitchen Towel, measuring
66.5cm × 50cm (26½in × 20in):

*Kitchen towel with two 9.5cm × 52.5cm
(3¾in × 21in) white 8-count Aida panels with red
edging (for suppliers, see page 48)
Stranded embroidery cotton in the colours given in
the panel
No24 tapestry needle
White sewing thread*

THE EMBROIDERY

Prepare the towel by machine zigzag stitching
around the raw edges to prevent fraying. Mark the
centre of each panel with lines of horizontal and
vertical basting stitches and mount in a hoop or
frame as shown on pages 4-5.

Following the chart and working on one panel of
the towel at a time, start to embroider from the
centre of the design, using four strands of cotton in
the needle. Gently steam press the finished
embroidery on the wrong side.

FINISHING THE TOWEL

Turn under a 12mm (½in) hem around all the edges
of the towel and then machine stitch using white
sewing thread.

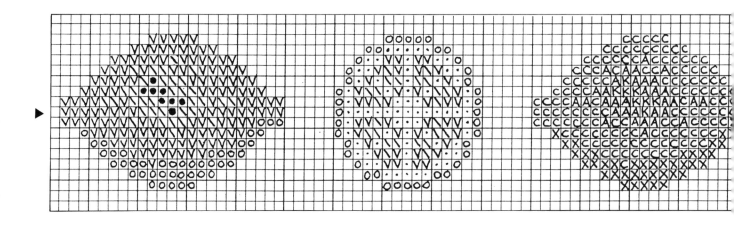

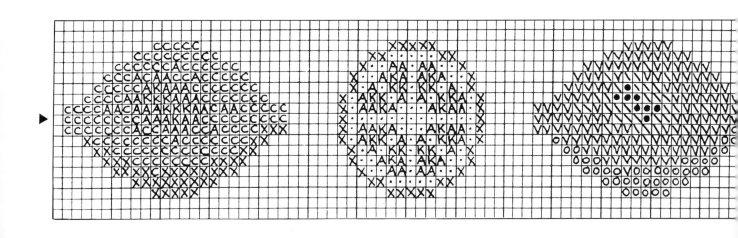

CITRUS KITCHEN ▼			
TOWEL	DMC	ANCHOR	MADEIRA
• Ecru	Ecru	387	Ecru
X Darkest green	987	244	1403
C Green	988	243	1402
A Pale green	3348	264	1409
K Palest green	472	278	1414
V Yellow	726	295	0100
O Darkest yellow	725	306	0108
\ Pale yellow	727	293	0110
● Palest yellow	3078	292	0102

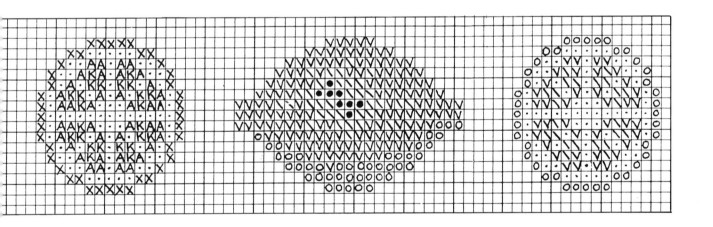

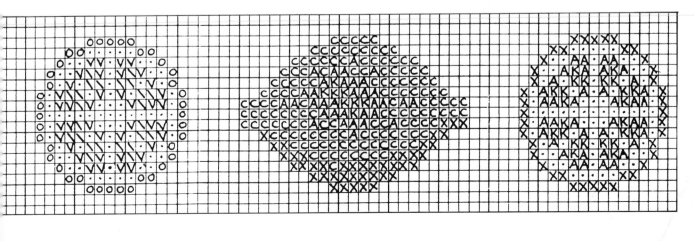

Vegetable Tea Towel

From carrots to peas, and peppers to sweetcorn, everyone's favourite vegetable is included in this decorative tea towel. If you can't bear to use the towel for drying the dishes, hang it on the kitchen wall!

VEGETABLE TEA TOWEL

YOU WILL NEED

For the Vegetable Tea Towel, measuring
51.5cm × 36.5cm (20½in × 14½in):

*60cm × 44cm (24in × 17½in) white Aida block
fabric (blocks of 11-count Aida fabric interwoven
with 22-block Hardanger fabric)
Stranded embroidery cotton in the colours given
in the panel
No24 tapestry needle
White sewing thread*

THE EMBROIDERY

Prepare the fabric by marking the centre of each Aida square to be stitched (see the diagram below) with horizontal and vertical lines of basting stitches. Then mount the fabric in a hoop or frame as shown on pages 4-5. Following the chart and starting from the centre of each design, embroider each motif using three strands of cotton in the needle for cross stitches. Work the backstitch details using two strands of cotton in the needle.

After completing the central motifs, stitch the border. Start from the corner, counting in three blocks diagonally from the corner edge to ensure correct placement. Gently steam press the finished embroidery on the wrong side.

FINISHING THE TEA TOWEL

Trim the edges of the fabric to within 3cm (1¼in) of the embroidery and machine zigzag stitch around all the edges to prevent fraying. Turn under 12mm (½in) around all the edges and press. Then machine straight stitch the hem in place.

	VEGETABLE TEA TOWEL ▶	DMC	ANCHOR	MADEIRA
⋀	Rich brown	434	365	2009
◇	Darkest green	3345	268	1406
A	Apple green	471	265	1501
B	Purple	327	100	0805
●	Light purple	917	89	0706
Z	Mushroom	613	853	2109
·	Ecru	Ecru	387	Ecru
T	Red	349	13	0212
N	Brown	611	898	2107
S	Golden brown	436	363	2011
M	Dark orange	921	338	0311
V	Orange	922	337	0310
O	Dark green	987	244	1403
P	Light green	989	242	1401
=	Green	988	243	1402
Y	Yellow	726	295	0100
O	Dark yellow	725	306	0108
W	Salmon pink	351	10	0214

Note: backstitch onion roots in rich brown, beetroot tip in purple, and pea tendrils in dark green.

HEM LINE

BORDER

| 5 | 8 |
| 3 |
| 4 | 6 |
| 7 |
| 1 | 2 |

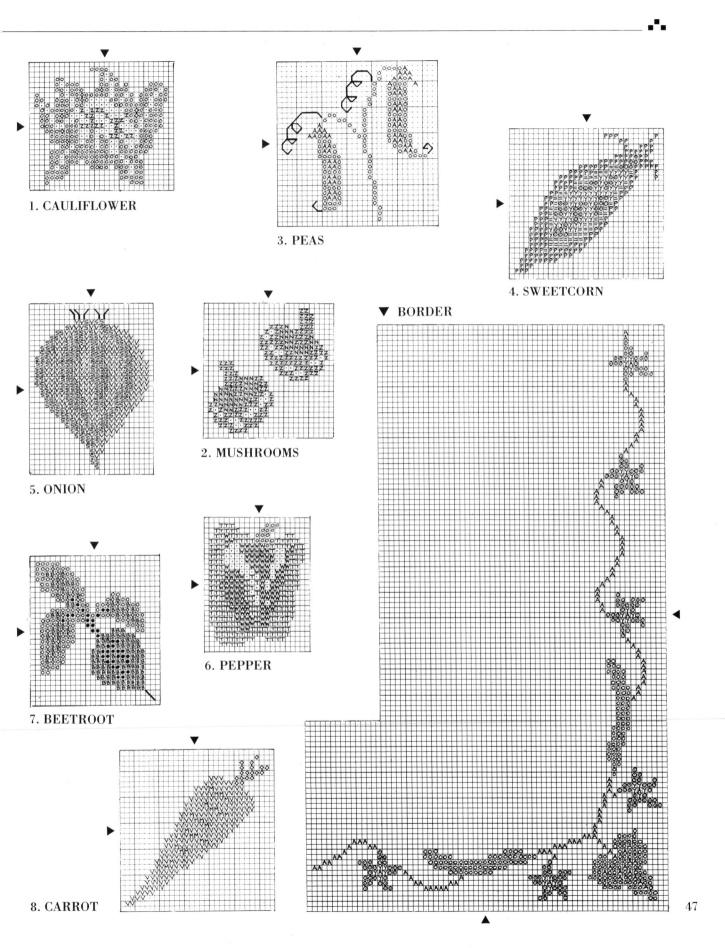

1. CAULIFLOWER

3. PEAS

4. SWEETCORN

5. ONION

2. MUSHROOMS

▼ BORDER

6. PEPPER

7. BEETROOT

8. CARROT

ACKNOWLEDGEMENTS

Special thanks are due to Tracy Medway for stitching the Fruit Garden Sampler, to Rowena for 'the bowl of my dreams', and of course to Cliff for charting the designs.

SUPPLIERS

The following mail order companies have supplied some of the basic items needed for making up the projects in this book:

Framecraft Miniatures Limited
372-376 Summer Lane
Hockley
Birmingham B19 3QA
Telephone: (021) 212 0551

Sew It All
Garden Cottage
Oving
Buckinghamshire
Telephone: (0296) 641524

Addresses for Framecraft stockists worldwide
Ireland Needlecraft Pty Ltd
2-4 Keppel Drive
Hallam, Victoria 3803
Australia

Danish Art Needlework
PO Box 442, Lethbridge
Alberta T1J 3Z1
Canada

Sanyei Imports
PO Box 5, Hashima Shi
Gifu 501-62
Japan

The Embroidery Shop
286 Queen Street
Masterton
New Zealand

Anne Brinkley Designs Inc
246 Walnut Street
Newton
Mass. 02160
USA

SA Threads and Cottons Ltd
43 Somerset Road
Cape Town
South Africa

For information on your nearest stockist of embroidery cotton, contact the following:

DMC

UK
DMC Creative World Limited
62 Pullman Road
Wigston, Leicester LE8 2DY
Telephone: 0533 811040

USA
The DMC Corporation
Port Kearney Bld
10 South Kearney
NJ 07032-0650
Telephone: 201 589 0606

AUSTRALIA
DMC Needlecraft Pty
PO Box 317
Earlswood 2206
NSW 2204
Telephone: 02599 3088

COATS AND ANCHOR

UK
Kilncraigs Mill
Alloa
Clackmannanshire
Scotland FK10 1EG
Telephone: 0259 723431

USA
Coats & Clark
PO Box 27067
Dept CO1
Greenville
SC 29616
Telephone: 803 234 0103

AUSTRALIA
Coats Patons Crafts
Thistle Street
Launceston
Tasmania 7250
Telephone: 00344 4222

MADEIRA

UK
Madeira Threads (UK) Limited
Thirsk Industrial Park
York Road, Thirsk
N. Yorkshire YO7 3BX
Telephone: 0845 524880

USA
Madeira Marketing Limited
600 East 9th Street
Michigan City
IN 46360
Telephone: 219 873 1000

AUSTRALIA
Penguin Threads Pty Limited
25-27 Izett Street
Prahran
Victoria 3181
Telephone: 03529 4400